CHIMPANZEE NESTS

Nature's Engineers

Christopher Forest

MEDIA ENHANCED BOOKS
AV2 BY WEIGL
ADDED VALUE • AUDIO VISUAL

www.av2books.com

MEDIA ENHANCED BOOKS
AV2 BY WEIGL™
ADDED VALUE • AUDIO VISUAL

Go to www.av2books.com, and enter this book's unique code.

BOOK CODE

A V E 2 8 6 7 2

AV² by Weigl brings you media enhanced books that support active learning.

AV² provides enriched content that supplements and complements this book. Weigl's AV² books strive to create inspired learning and engage young minds in a total learning experience.

Your AV² Media Enhanced books come alive with...

Audio
Listen to sections of the book read aloud.

Key Words
Study vocabulary, and complete a matching word activity.

Video
Watch informative video clips.

Quizzes
Test your knowledge.

Embedded Weblinks
Gain additional information for research.

Slide Show
View images and captions, and prepare a presentation.

Try This!
Complete activities and hands-on experiments.

... and much, much more!

Published by AV² by Weigl
350 5th Avenue, 59th Floor
New York, NY 10118
Website: www.av2books.com

Library of Congress Cataloging-in-Publication Data

Names: Forest, Christopher, author.
Title: Chimpanzee nests / Christopher Forest.
Description: New York, NY : AV2 by Weigl, [2019] | Series: Nature's engineers | Audience: K to Grade 3. | Includes bibliographical references and index.
Identifiers: LCCN 2018053470 (print) | LCCN 2018054189 (ebook) | ISBN 9781489697639 (Multi User ebook) | ISBN 9781489697646 (Single User ebook) | ISBN 9781489697615 (hardcover : alk. paper) | ISBN 9781489697622 (softcover : alk. paper)
Subjects: LCSH: Chimpanzees--Habitations--Juvenile literature.
Classification: LCC QL737.P94 (ebook) | LCC QL737.P94 F67 2019 (print) | DDC 599.885--dc23
LC record available at https://lccn.loc.gov/2018053470

Printed in Guangzhou, China
1 2 3 4 5 6 7 8 9 0 23 22 21 20 19

012019
102318

Project Coordinator: Heather Kissock
Art Director: Terry Paulhus

Photo Credits
Every reasonable effort has been made to trace ownership and to obtain permission to reprint copyright material. The publishers would be pleased to have any errors or omissions brought to their attention so that they may be corrected in subsequent printings.

Weigl acknowledges Getty Images, Alamy, Minden Pictures, iStock, and Shutterstock as its primary image suppliers for this title.

First published by North Star Editions in 2019.

CHIMPANZEE NESTS
Nature's Engineers

CONTENTS

ASLEEP IN THE LEAVES

A chimpanzee sits on a branch. She is high up in a tree. The chimp gathers leaves from the branch. Then, she climbs a little higher. She stops at a nest made of branches. She places the leaves in the nest. The leaves will make a soft place for her to sleep.

FUN FACT

A chimpanzee nest is approximately 3 feet (0.9 meters) wide.

Chimpanzees are active mainly during the day. They sleep in nests at night. The nests give the chimps shelter. They help the chimps stay warm. And they keep them safe from **predators**.

A chimp sleeps in a nest for eight to nine hours. When the Sun comes up, the chimp leaves the nest. The chimp spends some time in trees. It may also climb back down to the ground. The next night, it will build a new nest.

CHAPTER 2

BENDING BRANCHES

Most chimpanzees build nests high in trees. Some chimps climb more than 30 feet (9.1 m) above the ground. They bend and break tree branches to form a circle. These branches are the base of the nest.

FUN FACT

A chimpanzee weighs between 70 and 130 pounds (32 and 59 kilograms).

Some chimps bend branches in a triangle shape around this base. These branches give the base extra support. They make the nest strong and **stable**. The nest must not break while the chimp sleeps in it.

Next, chimps build the main part of the nest. They gather sticks, branches, and leaves. They weave the sticks and branches together. The weaving makes it difficult for the chimps to fall out of the nest while they sleep.

Chimpanzees look for branches that are stiff but **flexible**. These branches help make the nest strong. But they are also easy to bend and shape. It is easy for chimps to weave them together.

Then, chimps put leaves and twigs inside the nest. They line the nest's sides and bottom. Chimps rest their heads on the soft leaves. The leaves also help the chimps stay warm.

Chimps in warm areas use just a few leaves and twigs. But chimps in cooler regions add more. The leaves and twigs keep them warm at night.

FUN FACT

A chimpanzee takes approximately 10 minutes to build a nest.

AWAY FROM DANGER

Chimpanzees share their **habitat** with predators. Chimps try to build their nests far away from predators. One way they do this is by building nests high above the ground.

Leopards and other wild cats hunt **primates** such as chimpanzees. Many wild cats can climb trees. Chimps that live near wild cats build their nests higher up. However, some wild cats can still reach the nests.

The nests also protect chimps from pests. Biting and stinging insects tend to stay close to the ground. But chimpanzee nests are high in trees. For this reason, chimps in nests get fewer bites and stings.

Chimpanzees teach their babies how to build nests. At first, a baby chimp shares a nest with its mother. The mother cares for her baby. And she builds a new nest each day. A young chimp watches its mother. It learns how to build nests.

Eventually, the young chimp will leave its mother. Most chimps live on their own. But chimps of similar ages sometimes build nests close together. They help one another watch for danger.

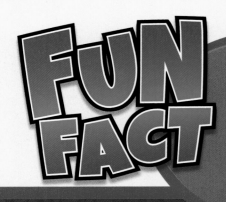

FUN FACT

A baby chimpanzee rides on its mother's back until it is two years old.

A CLOSER LOOK

THE BEST TREES

Chimpanzees build nests in several types of trees. Many chimps choose to make nests in Muhimbi trees. That is because these trees' leaves and branches are great for making nests.

A Muhimbi tree's branches are shaped like an upside-down **tripod**. This shape provides support for the chimpanzee. In addition, each branch has many leaves. The leaves serve as soft padding for the chimp's nest. Plus, there is not much space between the leaves. Leaves that are close together make great **insulation**.

REBUILD OR REUSE

Chimpanzees live in the forests and **savannas** of Africa. They can be found in Senegal, Uganda, and Tanzania. Sometimes, chimps hurt trees in these countries. They may break branches to build nests. Chimps also bend and weave branches. As a result, the branches may grow in unusual directions. This can hurt the tree.

However, chimps often reuse material. They take part of an old nest. They use the pieces to build a new nest nearby. In this way, they do less damage to trees.

Chimps eat from fruit trees. The chimps often stay close to the same trees. They may rebuild nests near these trees. Occasionally, they even use the same nest again.

FUN FACT

A chimp may build as many as 19,000 nests during its lifetime.

FUN FACT

Most chimpanzee nests break down within six months after they are built.

The greatest **threat** to the trees comes from humans. People have cleared trees to make roads, farms, and buildings. They have cut down much of the forests where chimps once lived. This is one reason chimpanzees are **endangered**.

Chimpanzee nests can help other animals. Insects and spiders move into a nest after a chimp has left. Chimps usually leave behind waste. This is one reason they build new nests almost every day. Insects eat this waste. In this way, chimpanzee nests are an important part of nature.

THE CHIMPANZEE NESTS QUIZ

1 How wide are chimpanzee nests?

2 How high do chimps climb above the ground?

3 How much do chimpanzees weigh?

4 How long does it take a chimpanzee to build a nest?

5 What kind of animals hunt chimpanzees?

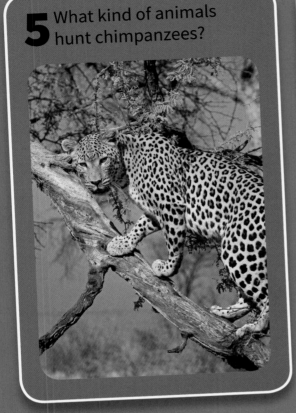

6 How long do baby chimpanzees ride on their mother's backs?

7 Chimps choose to make nests in which type of tree?

8 In which three countries do chimpanzees live?

ANSWERS

1. Approximately 3 feet (0.9 meters) **2.** More than 30 feet (9.1 m) **3.** Between 70 and 130 pounds (32 and 59 kilograms) **4.** 10 minutes **5.** Wild cats **6.** Until they are 2 years old **7.** The Muhimbi tree **8.** Senegal, Uganda, and Tanzania

KEY WORDS

endangered: in danger of dying out

flexible: easy to bend or change

habitat: the type of place where plants or animals normally grow or live

insulation: material that covers something and keeps heat from getting in or out

predators: animals that hunt other animals for food

primates: mammals with hands that can grasp things

savannas: grasslands with few or no trees

stable: unlikely to move, break, or change

threat: something that can cause danger or harm

tripod: a stand with three legs that is used to hold objects

INDEX

Log on to www.av2books.com

AV² by Weigl brings you media enhanced books that support active learning. Go to www.av2books.com, and enter the special code found on page 2 of this book. You will gain access to enriched and enhanced content that supplements and complements this book. Content includes video, audio, weblinks, quizzes, a slide show, and activities.

AV² Online Navigation

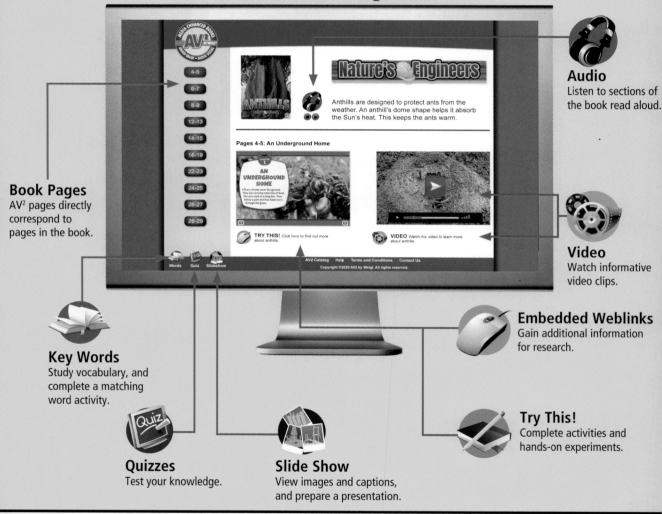

Audio
Listen to sections of the book read aloud.

Book Pages
AV² pages directly correspond to pages in the book.

Video
Watch informative video clips.

Key Words
Study vocabulary, and complete a matching word activity.

Embedded Weblinks
Gain additional information for research.

Quizzes
Test your knowledge.

Slide Show
View images and captions, and prepare a presentation.

Try This!
Complete activities and hands-on experiments.

AV² was built to bridge the gap between print and digital. We encourage you to tell us what you like and what you want to see in the future.

Sign up to be an AV² Ambassador at www.av2books.com/ambassador.